D1408128

DESTINATION
THE MOON

GILES SPARROW

PowerKiDS
press

New York

Published in 2010 by The Rosen Publishing Group
29 East 21st Street, New York, NY 10010

U.S. Editor: Kara Murray

Picture Credits
Key: t – top, b – below, c – center, l – left, r – right. iStockphoto: Alexandra
Draghici 19l, 19r; Lockheed Martin Corp: 6-7; LPI: USRA 2-3, 8-9, 15; NASA: 8, 9, 12-
13, 18, 22-23, 28t, 29, GSFC 12c, 13, 14, 25tr, 27b, JPL TP, 2, 10-11, KSC 26, MSFC
28b; Science Photo Library: Mark Garlick 16-17, Ria Novosti 25tl, 27t; Shutterstock:
Kevin Carden 24-25, Michiel de Boer 21, George Toubalis 4, Vladimir Wrangel 20-21,
Vladimir Zivkovic 7

Front cover: NASA: bl, JPL (c); Back cover: NASA: JP; Backgrounds: NASA

Library of Congress Cataloging-in-Publication Data

Sparrow, Giles.
  Destination the moon / Giles Sparrow. — 1st ed.
     p. cm. — (Destination solar system)
  Includes index.
  ISBN 978-1-4358-3445-3 (lib. bdg.) — ISBN 978-1-4358-3465-1 (pbk.) —
ISBN 978-1-4358-3466-8 (6-pack)
  1. Moon—Juvenile literature. I. Title.
  QB582.S678 2010
  523.3—dc22

                                         2009005275

Manufactured in China

CONTENTS

>>>>>>>   >>>>>>>

WHERE IS THE MOON?

The Moon is our nearest neighbor in space, it is right next to us compared to the other objects in the **solar system**.

The Moon is our natural **satellite**, held in **orbit** around Earth by the force of **gravity**. It goes around Earth every 27 days.

Imagine you are going on a **mission** to the Moon. The Moon is very near compared to the neighboring planets but your journey will still take several days. A powerful rocket could travel the distance from Earth to the Moon in less than ten hours, but your journey will take much longer—three whole days, in fact. You cannot travel in a straight

SIZE COMPARED TO EARTH

Moon's diameter: 2,159 miles (3,475 km)

Earth's diameter: 7,926 miles (12,756 km)

DISTANCE FROM EARTH

This diagram shows the distance from the Moon to Earth. The Moon is about 30 Earth-widths from Earth. It is the only large satellite orbiting Earth.

Earth

0

50,000 miles (80,000 km)

100,000 m (160,000 k

Moon

This artist's impression shows the planets of the inner solar system: Mercury, Venus, Earth, and Mars. You can also see the asteroid belt and the Moon as it orbits Earth.

...ne to the Moon. Instead, you have ...o travel in a figure-eight path that ...will put you into the correct orbit ...round the Moon. Also, you have to ...llow time for your spacecraft to ...peed up and then slow down.

...When you reach the halfway point to ...e Moon, your spacecraft will turn ...round and travel backwards. Small ...ockets on the craft will then begin ...iring to slow you down.

Getting to the Moon

The Moon is much closer to Earth than the nearest planets, yet it is still a great distance away. The time it takes to get there depends on how you travel.

Distance from Earth to the Moon

Closest	221,462 miles (356,410 km)
Farthest	252,698 miles (406,679 km)

By car at 70 miles per hour (113 km/h)

Closest	132 days
Farthest	150 days

By rocket at 7 miles per second (11 km/s)

Closest	9 hours
Farthest	10 hours

Time for radio signals to reach the Moon (at the speed of light)

Closest	1.19 seconds
Farthest	1.36 seconds

Moon

150,000 miles (240,000 km)	200,000 miles (320,000 km)	250,000 miles (400,000 km)

ON THE WAY

F rom Earth, the Moon is a beautiful sight. Along with the Sun, it is the largest object in the sky.

Your spacecraft is just the top part of a tall rocket. Most of the space in the rocket is taken up by the fuel tanks needed to send your craft into space.

SIZING UP

The Moon looks about the same size as the Sun. However, since it is 400 times smaller and also 400 times closer to Earth, the two objects only appear to be the same size from Earth. Unlike the Sun, the Moon shines only by reflecting sunlight.

CHANGING SHAPE

As the Moon moves around Earth, we see it lit from different angles, and this causes **lunar phases**. When the Moon lies between Earth and the Sun, the Sun shines on its far side, and we cannot see it. This is called a new moon. A week later, the Moon has moved so that half the visible side is sunlit—this is the first quarter. By the next week, the Moon is opposite the Sun and its Earth-facing side is flooded with sunlight—this is a full moon.

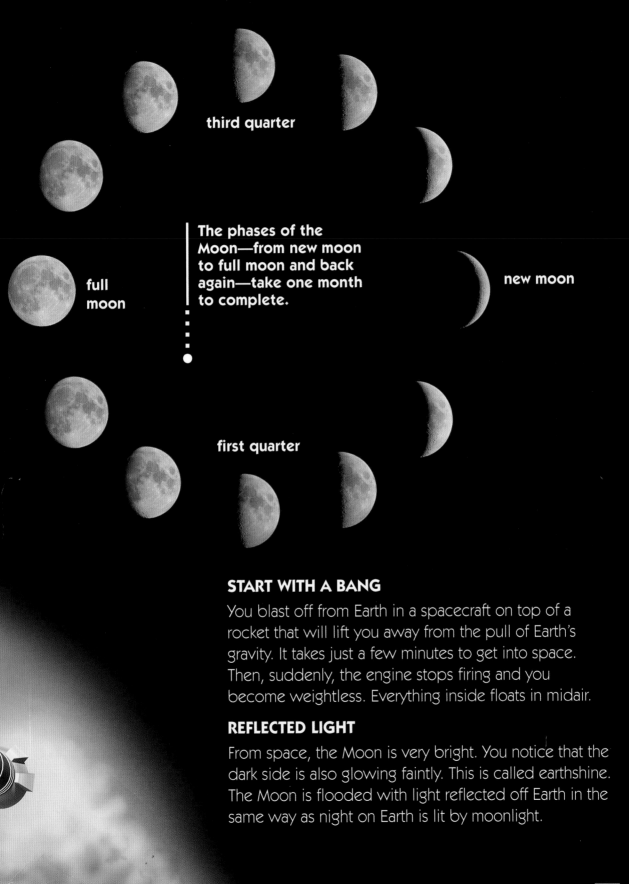

third quarter

full moon

The phases of the Moon—from new moon to full moon and back again—take one month to complete.

new moon

first quarter

START WITH A BANG

You blast off from Earth in a spacecraft on top of a rocket that will lift you away from the pull of Earth's gravity. It takes just a few minutes to get into space. Then, suddenly, the engine stops firing and you become weightless. Everything inside floats in midair.

REFLECTED LIGHT

From space, the Moon is very bright. You notice that the dark side is also glowing faintly. This is called earthshine. The Moon is flooded with light reflected off Earth in the same way as night on Earth is lit by moonlight.

SURFACE

Leaving your main spacecraft in orbit, you board a lander to visit the Moon's surface.

TOUCH DOWN

You steer toward an area of rolling hills, carefully avoiding **crater** edges or steep slopes that might be **dangerous** to land on. It is a smooth ride because the Moon has no wind to blow your spacecraft around.

As you get close to the ground, the blast of your rockets whips up a cloud of fine dust. Will the ground be firm enough to take your weight? The engine stops just above the surface and you drop down with a bump. There is another puff of dust, but you do not sink into it.

MOON WALKING

The Moon's weak gravity is just one-sixth of that on Earth. You cannot wait to get outside and jump around on the surface. As you step outside in your space suit, the soil crumbles beneath your boots. You reach down and pick some up, it seems to be a mixture of ground-up rocks of all sizes.

The Moon is covered in a thick layer of rock dust and a few large stones.

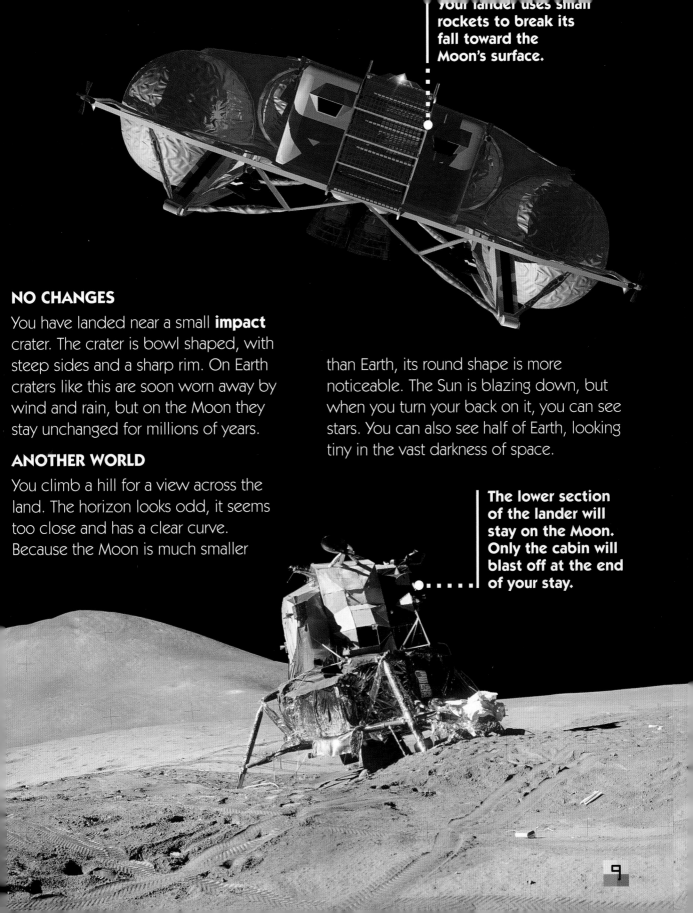

Your lander uses small rockets to break its fall toward the Moon's surface.

NO CHANGES

You have landed near a small **impact** crater. The crater is bowl shaped, with steep sides and a sharp rim. On Earth craters like this are soon worn away by wind and rain, but on the Moon they stay unchanged for millions of years.

ANOTHER WORLD

You climb a hill for a view across the land. The horizon looks odd, it seems too close and has a clear curve. Because the Moon is much smaller than Earth, its round shape is more noticeable. The Sun is blazing down, but when you turn your back on it, you can see stars. You can also see half of Earth, looking tiny in the vast darkness of space.

The lower section of the lander will stay on the Moon. Only the cabin will blast off at the end of your stay.

9

SEAS AND CRATERS

Y ou return in the lander to your spacecraft and fly a few hundred feet (m) above the Moon's surface, studying the landscape.

FLAT PLAIN

You are traveling over a great plain of bare rock. This is the Sea of Tranquillity. The first people to make maps of the Moon thought these dark plains looked like oceans of water.

Because the Moon's seas do not have any water, they are called **maria** instead. This is the Latin word for "sea." The cratered areas between the seas are called **terrae**.

SHADOW SCENE

You are approaching the **terminator** now. This is the line that divides night from day on the Moon. As the Sun sinks in the sky behind you, the shadows it casts grow longer, revealing more landscape details. The surface is not entirely flat. In some places it is wrinkled or cracked. A strange, snakelike valley called a **rill** stretches across it.

Plato

Sea of Rains

Ocean of Storms

Copernicus

Sea of Clouds

Tycho

ROCK SAMPLE

You land to collect some rocks from the plain. The lunar seas are made of basalt, an iron-rich rock that is also common on Earth. Basalt forms when **molten** rock cools down quickly, so the lunar seas must have formed from floods of **lava**.

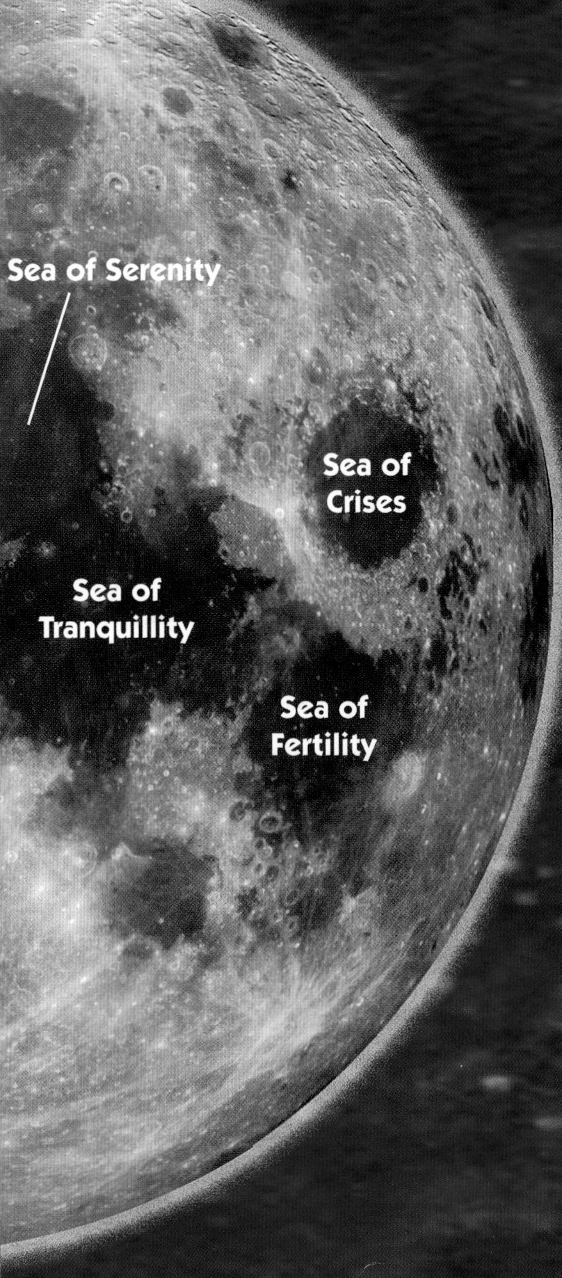

Sea of Serenity

Sea of Crises

Sea of Tranquillity

Sea of Fertility

HOW THE MARIA FORMED

The lunar seas, or maria, formed from huge floods of lava. The lava erupted from inside the Moon millions of years ago and swept across the surface, as shown below. The maria have few craters so they must have formed after the craters that cover the rest of the Moon. Some of the biggest craters, called basins, are filled in with maria. The wrinkles are a result of the maria distorting as they pushed down on the crust below. The rills are channels along which lava once flowed.

Cratered surface before lava flood

Lava forms flat sea

SANDY ROCKS

Next you visit a highland region. The highlands cover most of the Moon's surface and appear much brighter than the dark maria. You land to take some more rock **samples**. The highland rocks turn out to be a mixture of feldspar and silica. On Earth feldspar is found in many rocks and clay. Silica is the main **mineral** in sand.

The highland regions rise out of the lunar maria like islands poking out above the ocean on Earth.

MOON DUST

The entire surface of the Moon is covered in dust called regolith. This was formed over millions of years as small meteorites smashed into rocks on the surface and crushed them into powder. Because the Moon has no wind or water to wear down its surface, this astronaut's footprint in the regolith could last for millions of years.

NO PROTECTION

The highlands are more heavily cratered than the maria. Most pieces of space rock burn up as they enter Earth's **atmosphere**, turning into shooting stars. Only very large **meteorites** make it to the ground and produce craters. On the Moon there is no atmosphere, so everything from giant **comets** to tiny specks of dust hits the surface and leaves a crater.

CRATER CLOCK

The Moon has no weather, so craters are not worn away by wind and rain. As a result **astronomers** can tell the age of different parts of the Moon's surface simply by counting the craters. The older regions have more craters.

SMASHING TIME

Most of the craters on the Moon are 3.9 billion years old. A storm of impacts created the jumbled landscape that covers the highlands today. About 3.85 billion years ago, the Moon received some huge impacts. These produced gigantic craters, or **basins**.

The Copernicus crater is 800 million years old, 3,250 feet (1 km) deep, and 60 miles (97 km) across.

TO THE FAR SIDE

From Earth, we can see only one side of the Moon. You decide to take a look at the far side for the first time. As you steer your ship around the Moon, you see Earth sinking below the horizon behind you—your first earthset!

ROUGH SURFACE

The far side of the Moon is covered with deep craters, and there are almost no maria. Your spaceship's instruments show that the ground is rougher there than on the visible side. There is a 10-mile (16 km) difference between the tallest hills and deepest valleys. That is the same as the distance from Earth's deep ocean floor to the top of Mount Everest.

GIANT CRATER

Near the south **pole**, you see a colossal crater that is surrounded by a wall of mountains. This is the South Pole-Aitken Basin. It is the biggest impact crater known to science and is more than 1,550 miles (2,500 km) across. Its bottom is scattered with other craters. Some are so deep that their bases never see the Sun.

The far side of the Moon never faces Earth, but it is a mistake to think that it is always dark. The Sun shines on it as much as it does on the near side.

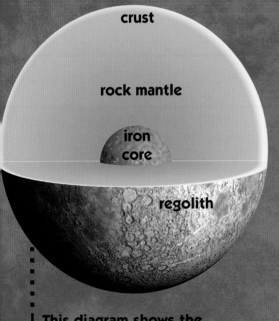

crust

rock mantle

iron
core

regolith

This diagram shows the internal structure of the Moon. The regolith is several miles (km) deep!

The surface of the Moon is regularly shaken by **moonquakes**. Your instruments can use these quakes to find out what the Moon is made of and how it formed.

SHAKY GROUND

Some moonquakes are caused by the pull of Earth's gravity. Others are shock waves from the steady stream of meteorites that hit the Moon. As the shock waves pass through the different layers inside the Moon, they speed up or slow down. Astronomers can measure the waves to map the inside of the Moon.

LAYERED STRUCTURE

Beneath the **regolith** is a layer of broken rocks. Then there is a solid **crust**, reaching down about 45 miles (72 km). Below the crust is a **mantle** of solid rock. No one is sure how far down the mantle goes. It might make up the whole of the Moon or there might be a **core** of solid iron.

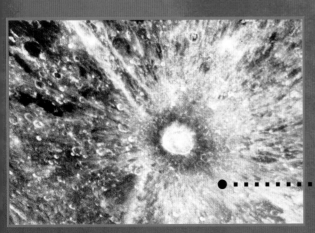

Bright rays surrounding craters are made up of rocks blasted out from deep under ground by the impact.

SAME MATERIAL

Your rock samples show that the Moon is made of some minerals that are also found on Earth. This suggests that the Moon and Earth formed together. However, the Moon's rocks do not have many metals in them.

BIG SMASH

Today nearly all astronomers agree that the Moon was formed in an enormous collision. At some point in the history of Earth, long before life had begun, our planet may have collided with another planet about the size of Mars. The enormous explosion **vaporized** huge amounts of both planets and blasted **debris** into orbit. Lighter materials from their crusts and mantles ended up in orbit, while the iron cores of the two planets merged together.

NEW MOON

After the collision, Earth's surface cooled down, forming a thinner crust than before. The material left in orbit began to stick together, building up to form the Moon. The Moon could have formed in just a few years.

This artist's impression shows how the Moon formed from rock smashed off the Earth by an impact with a small planet.

A DOUBLE PLANET

The Moon and Earth are sometimes called a double planet. Earth's Moon is the largest in the solar system when compared to the size of its parent planet.

PULLING TOGETHER

Earth and the Moon have a large effect on each other. The clearest effect of the Moon on Earth is the tides, which are caused by the Moon's gravity pulling on Earth's ocean water.

FIXED POSITION

The Earth's **tidal forces** also act on the Moon. The constant tug of Earth's gravity slowed down the Moon's rotation until it had one side always locked toward us. The Moon now makes one full rotation for each orbit around Earth.

Earth's gravity may also explain why maria formed mostly on the near side of the Moon. When the Moon was young, its mantle was molten. The heavy materials in the mantle were pulled toward Earth by its gravity, making eruptions much more likely on the near side of the Moon.

The Moon does not orbit around Earth's exact center. Instead it moves around a point 1,060 miles (1,706 km) under the planet's surface.

DRIFTING APART

Earth's tidal forces are changing the Moon's orbit. The Moon gets about 1.2 inches (3 cm) farther from Earth every year and takes slightly longer to travel around its orbit. At the same time, the pull of the Moon on Earth is slowing our planet's rotation gradually and making our days longer. About 300 million years ago, a day on Earth was only 21 hours long!

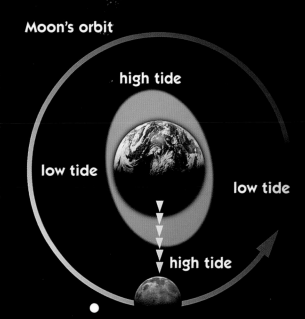

Moon's orbit

high tide

low tide

low tide

high tide

High tides are caused by the Moon's gravity pulling on the ocean, making a bulge that sweeps around the globe as Earth spins each day. The bulge near the Moon is balanced by another on the far side of Earth.

The difference between low and high tide can be many feet (m). The highest tides occur when the Moon's gravity is added to by the Sun's.

(1)

(2)

DAY BECOMES NIGHT

When the Moon passes directly over the Sun's face, it creates one of nature's most spectacular special effects—a total solar **eclipse**. Day turns into night in a matter of seconds, and the air grows suddenly cold. Then, as quickly as it began, the eclipse is over, and the Sun reappears and lights up the world.

This sequence of images shows the effect of a lunar eclipse as Earth's shadow gradually covers the Moon.

NARROW VIEW

A solar eclipse happens every one or two years, but you need to be in the correct place to see it. When the Moon's small shadow crosses Earth, it creates a track thousands of miles (km) long but only a few miles (km) wide. Only people in this strip of land see the

SHADOW PLAY

During a solar eclipse (1, left), the Moon moves in front of the Sun, blocking its view from Earth. The shadow cast by the Moon races across Earth, and the eclipse is over within minutes. A total eclipse can be seen only within the Moon's shadow (dark purple), while those just outside the shadow will see a partial eclipse. A lunar eclipse (2), when Earth passes between the Sun and the Moon, lasts a lot longer because Earth's shadow is so much larger.

total eclipse. As a result, any one place on Earth will experience a total solar eclipse just once every few hundred years.

RED MOON

When Earth casts its shadow on the Moon, a lunar eclipse occurs. These happen about once a year, and anyone with a view of the Moon can see it.

The Moon does not disappear during a lunar eclipse, it just turns dark red (pictured below). This is because Earth's shadow does not have a sharp edge. Some hazy red sunlight gets through our atmosphere.

A DAY ON
THE MOON

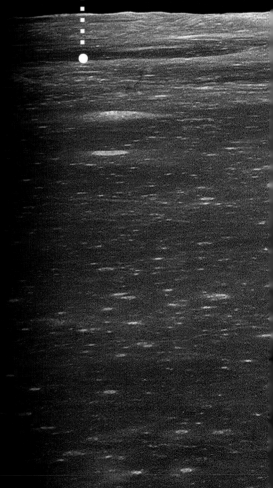

A full day on the Moon, from one sunrise to the next, lasts about 29 Earth days.

A VIEW OF EARTH

Standing on the side of the Moon nearest Earth, you can see your home planet hanging in the sky. It is almost four times the size of a full moon seen from Earth. On most of the near side, Earth is always up and does not move much in the Moon's sky. However, on the edges between the far and near side, a wobble in the Moon's rotation means Earth slowly rises and sets from time to time. As you watch, the Sun rises slowly in the east. It will take nearly 14 Earth days to move across the Moon's sky before setting in the west.

EXTREME TEMPERATURES

Because there is no atmosphere to shield the Moon from the Sun's rays, the surface can reach 230 °F (110 °C) during the day. This is hotter than boiling water. Fortunately your space suit keeps you cool in the daytime and warm at night, when the temperature can fall as low as −292 °F (−180 °C).

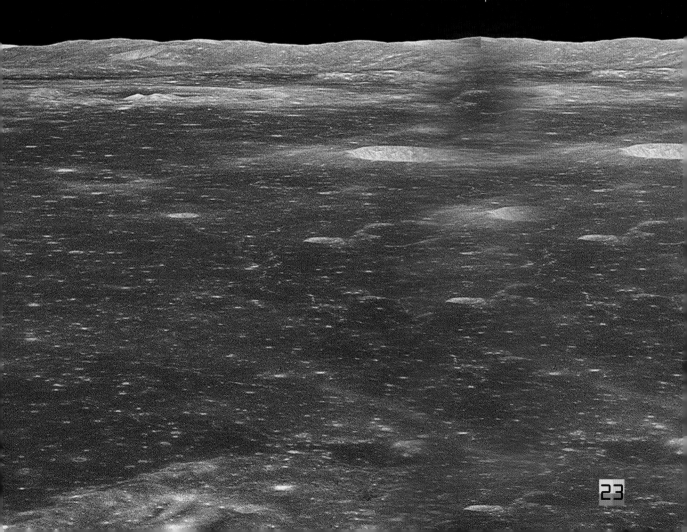

MOONQUAKE TIME

Throughout the long day, your quake detectors are operating. They show that moonquakes reach a peak roughly every 14 Earth days. This puzzles you for a while, but then you figure out the reason. Moonquakes are most violent when the Moon is closest to and farthest away from Earth. This is when the tidal forces produced by Earth's gravity reach their peak.

NIGHT ON THE MOON

Night falls quickly on the Moon because there is no atmosphere to create twilight. Sunlight reflected from Earth stops the lunar night from becoming pitch-black. Looking in the opposite direction from Earth, you can see millions of stars in the sky—many more than are visible from beneath Earth's atmosphere.

FLYING
TO THE MOON

A s our nearest neighbor, the Moon has a special place in our myths and beliefs. In 1969, the Moon became special for another reason when it was visited by people.

MOON WATCHERS

The Moon has always been used to measure time. The 12 months in our year are based on the 29-day lunar cycle, the time between new moons.

Because the Moon is so close to Earth, astronomers began to understand the things it did long before they knew much about the rest of the solar system. They saw that the Moon orbited Earth, and they supposed everything else did as well!

People could see the maria and some faint patterns on the lunar surface with the naked eye. Early telescopes revealed the maria were dry plains, and the Moon also had mountains, valleys, and craters. The first detailed maps of the Moon were drawn in the late 1800s, and

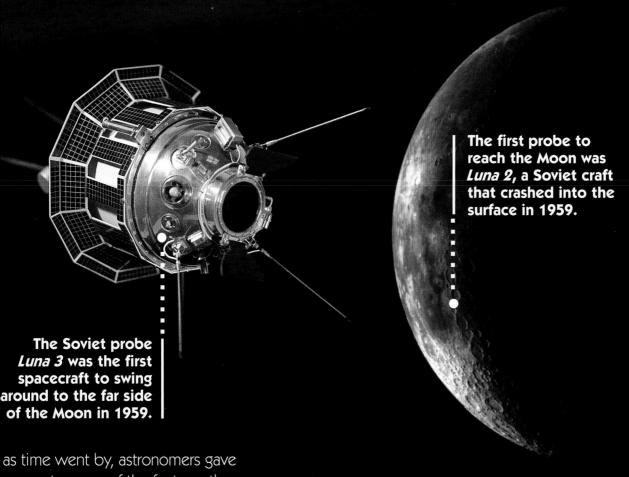

The first probe to reach the Moon was *Luna 2*, a Soviet craft that crashed into the surface in 1959.

The Soviet probe *Luna 3* was the first spacecraft to swing around to the far side of the Moon in 1959.

as time went by, astronomers gave names to more of the features they saw.

RACE TO THE MOON

When the United States and the **Soviet Union** sent the first satellites and **astronauts** into space in the 1950s and 1960s, the Moon became the next place they wanted to go. The two nations were locked in a struggle for control of the world. They thought that if they could get to the Moon first, they might be able to control space, too. The **space race** began.

The Soviets took an early lead in 1959 by firing **probes** at and around the Moon. Then they ran out of luck, their next five Moon probes failed to land on the Moon. This gave **NASA** a chance to catch up.

Stonehenge in England was built 4,000 years ago to observe the movements of the Moon, Sun, and stars.

MISSION TO THE MOON

NASA sent Moon probes in three waves—the Rangers, the Lunar Orbiters, and the Surveyors. The first Ranger probes crashed into the Moon in 1964, sending back pictures before they hit the surfac[e]

The Lunar Orbiter and Surveyor programs ran between 1966 and 1968. The five Orbiters photographed 99 percent of the lunar surface, while the Surveyors made **soft landings** on the Moo[n] However, the Soviet *Luna 9* probe had beaten NASA to the first soft landing by four months. The probes proved that a landing on the Moon was possible. Until the astronomers had worried that landers might sink in the regolith.

APOLLO PROGRAM

NASA's crewed lunar missions were called the Apollo program. Astronauts trained in orbit aboard small spacecraft. Engineers on the ground created a larger spacecraf[t] to carry a crew of three to the Moon and land two of them on the surface.

The huge *Saturn V* rocket was made to lift three men and their spacecraft into space and then fire them at the Moon.

EAGLE HAS LANDED

On July 20, 1969, the *Apollo 11* lunar module (named *Eagle*) landed on the Moon, and astronauts Neil Armstrong and Edwin "Buzz" Aldrin stepped out onto the surface for the first time. Armstrong and Aldrin stayed for just a few hours, but later Apollo missions lasted much longer. Astronauts collected moon rocks, set up detectors to study moonquakes, and even took a lunar rover for a drive.

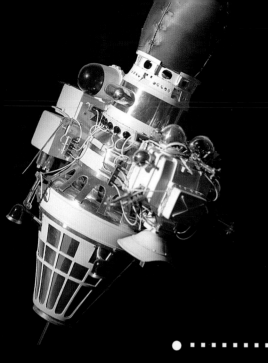

Luna 9 was the first spacecraft to make a soft landing on the Moon. The uncrewed lander was the upper section, which was blasted free just before the lower half hit the surface.

An astronaut inspects the Surveyor III probe on the Moon after landing in Apollo 12 in 1969.

This artist's impression shows the *Orion* module (top) docked with an *Altair* lander (bottom).

LAST MEN ON THE MOON

The Apollo program ended with *Apollo 17* in 1972. No human has been back to the Moon since then. The Soviets abandoned their plans for crewed lunar landings and sent several robot landers to collect rock samples and return them to Earth.

The next crew to fly to the Moon will travel in an *Orion* spacecraft, which has room for four people.

The crew will be sent off by a small *Ares I* rocket.

The *Altair* lander and other heavy gear will go in larger *Ares V* rockets and fly much of the way to the Moon by remote control.

The *Ares V* rocket will be even more powerful than the *Saturn V* rockets from the Apollo program.

WE SHALL RETURN

A few probes visited the Moon in the 1990s to look for minerals and map the Moon's surface. Then in 2004, U.S. president George W. Bush asked NASA to plan a return mission to the Moon as the first stage in crewed missions to Mars and perhaps other planets. This request became the Constellation program, which aims to put an astronaut on the Moon in 2020.

COULD HUMANS LIVE THERE?

One of the goals of the Constellation program is to set up a Moon base. People could be living on the Moon in 20 years!

AT HOME ON THE MOON

The NASA moon base will be called the Lunar Refuge. Astronauts could live there for several months. It would be relatively simple to construct an **airtight** building and provide it with supplies, crews, and gear using the Ares rockets. Water ice may be buried in the Moon's rocks or at the bottom of deep, cold craters. Ice could provide not just water and **oxygen**, but also **hydrogen**, which can be used as fuel.

The main danger to people at the base would be **radiation** from the Sun, but shields could be placed around the base, or the entire thing could be buried underground for protection. The lessons learned from living on the Moon would be valuable for planning a long stay on Mars.

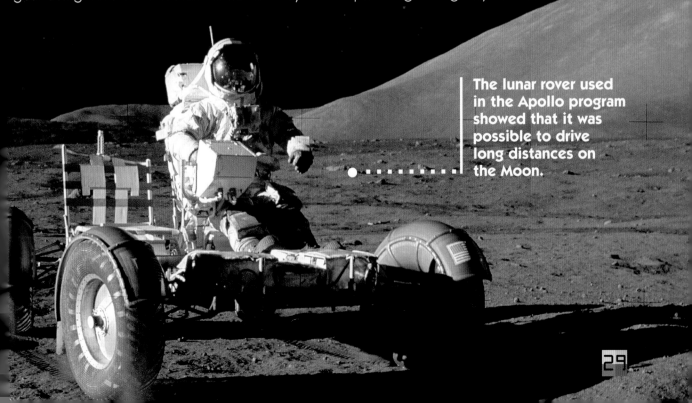

The lunar rover used in the Apollo program showed that it was possible to drive long distances on the Moon.

GLOSSARY

airtight (ER-tyt) Built so air cannot leak out.

astronauts (AS-truh-nots) People trained to go into space.

astronomers (uh-STRAH-nuh-merz) Scientists who study planets and other objects in space.

atmosphere (AT-muh-sfeer) A layer of gas trapped by gravity around the surface of a planet or moon.

basins (BAY-sinz) Large impact craters that filled up with lava.

comets (KAH-mits) Large chunks of ice left over from when the planets formed.

core (KOR) The center of a planet or moon.

crater (KRAY-tur) A hole made when an object from space crashes into a planet or moon.

crust (KRUST) The solid outer surface of a planet or moon.

dangerous (DAYN-jeh-rus) Able to cause harm.

debris (duh-BREE) Pieces of rock, dust, ice, or other material.

eclipse (ih-KLIPS) The effect caused by a planet or moon moving in front of the Sun and casting a shadow on another object.

gravity (GRA-vih-tee) The force that pulls objects together. The heavier or closer an object is, the stronger its gravity, or pull.

hydrogen (HY-dreh-jen) The simplest, lightest, and most common element in the universe.

impact (IM-pakt) When two objects hit each other.

lava (LAH-vuh) Molten rock on a planet's or moon's surface.

lunar (LOO-ner) Having to do with the Moon.

mantle (MAN-tul) The part of a planet or moon located between the core and the crust.

maria (singular mare) (MAHR-ee-uh) Smooth, dark plains created by huge floods of lava that swept across the surface of the Moon; also called seas.

meteorites (MEE-tee-uh-ryts) Space rocks that land on the surface of a planet or moon.

mineral (MIN-rul) A type of solid chemical found in rock.

mission (MIH-shun) An expedition to visit a specific place in space, such as a planet, moon, or asteroid.

molten (MOHL-ten) Hot and liquid.

moonquakes (MOON-kwayks) Like earthquakes, only they take place on the Moon.

NASA (NA-suh) The National Aeronautics and Space Administration, the U.S. space agency in charge of sending people and probes into space.

orbit (OR-bit) The path an object takes around a larger object.

oxygen (OK-sih-jen) The invisible gas in Earth's air that living things breathe in.

phases (FAYZ-ez) Areas of planets or moons that are lit by the Sun.

pole (POHL) A point on the surface of a planet that coincides with the top or bottom end of its axis.

probes (PROHBZ) Robotic vehicles sent from Earth to study the solar system.

radiation (ray-dee-AY-shun) Energy that comes out in rays from a source. Heat and light are types of radiation.

regolith (REH-guh-lith) The top layer of rocky soil on the Moon formed from meteorite impacts.

rill (RIL) A channel on the Moon that once carried lava.

samples (SAM-pulz) Small parts of thing that show what the rest is like.

satellite (SA-tih-lyt) An object that orbits a planet.

space race (SPAYS RAYS) The competition between the United States and the Soviet Union to explore space.

soft landings (SAWFT LAND-ingz) Controlled landings so the spacecraft is unharmed.

solar system (SOH-ler SIS-tem) The planets, asteroids, and comets that orbit the Sun.

Soviet Union (SOH-vee-et YOON-yun) An empire centered on Russia that ruled a huge area stretching from Europe to East Asia in the twentieth century.

terminator (TER-mih-nay-ter) The line that divides night from day on the Moon.

terrae (teh-RAY) Crater-covered highlands between the lunar maria.

tidal forces (TY-dul FORS-ez) The pulls on the surfaces of planets or moons caused by the gravity of another moon or planet nearby or by the Sun.

vaporized (VAY-puh-ryzd) Turned to gas.

INDEX

WEB SITES

Due to the changing nature of Internet links, PowerKids Press has developed
an online list of Web sites related to the subject of this book. This site is
updated regularly. Please use this link to access the list:
www.powerkidslinks.com/dsol/moon/